# Rocket!

Written by Karra McFarlane

**Collins**

Put on a thick jacket.

Get in the rocket.

4

Check it.

Then, the jets kick in.

# 3 … 2 … 1 … Bang!

The jets get the rocket up.

The rocket zips off.

Yes!

rocket

jets

# The rocket is quick!

It zips up!

13

14

# ✿ After reading ✿

**Letters and Sounds:** Phase 3

**Word count:** 40

**Focus phonemes:** /j/ /y/ /z/ zz /qu/ /ch/ /th/ /ng/

**Common exception words:** the, and, put

**Curriculum links:** Understanding the world

**Early learning goals:** Reading: read and understand simple sentences; use phonic knowledge to decode regular words and read them aloud accurately; read some common irregular words

## Developing fluency

- Your child may enjoy hearing you read the book.
- Ask your child to read the sentences with expression, emphasising the sentences that end with exclamation marks, and pausing – for suspense – at the ellipses (…) on page 7.

## Phonic practice

- On page 2, focus on **thick**. Ask your child to find the pairs of letters that each make one sound. (*"th" and "ck"*)
- Ask your child to find the two letters that make one sound in each of these words before reading them:

  check     then     fizz     off     rocket     quick

- On page 7, point to **Bang!** and ask your child which pairs of letters make one sound before asking them to read the sentence. (*"ng"*)
- Look at the "I spy sounds" pages (14 and 15) together. Point to the juice and say "juice", emphasising the /j/ sound. Point to the yogurt and say "yogurt", emphasising the /y/ sound. Challenge your child to find more words containing these sounds. (e.g. *jug, jam, jumper, yellow, yacht*)

## Extending vocabulary

- Point to **Bang!** on page 7 and **fizz!** on page 9. Ask your child if they can say the words so that they sound like their meaning. Can they think of other words and say them like they sound? (e.g. *whoosh, screech, tap tap, ping, crash*)
- Discuss the words that would best match the sounds of a rocket as it takes off, moves around Earth, lands on the moon, and then returns to Earth, splashing into the sea.